Word Gallery

By

Ayrene

WORD GALLERY

First edition. September 11, 2024.

ISBN: 979-8227880093

Written by Ayrene.

Poetry and prose, for me, are something I always turn to when I get devastated by reality.

Reading always therapies me when I feel insecure, vulnerable, betrayed, or even bored by the clichés things happening in my daily life.

As time passed by, I started to write and I've loved the difference between writing novels and poems. Writing novels can make me escape from the real world while writing poems makes me travel into my inner world - the meaningful place where I love to live in and keep myself sane.

There were times I stopped writing for a while and did not post anything much on my social media. Certain people asked me via my Instagram account when my book would get launched. Well, you have no idea how much that question means to me. That question was like fuel to get me through those hard times.

I, eventually, am launching my first book now. It is called Word Gallery. It has a lot of blank space on each page which I, myself, in the past wouldn't do because when I was a kid, I used to think that a book with a lot of blank pages was a waste of money.

From the past years, I've learned that the blank space allows me to connect with all the words and the meaning between the lines on those pages.

Every time I finish reading a verse, my mind will look toward my inner emotions and absorb all of the feelings being conveyed on the page. It is like a pause that allows me to explore my inner self.

I hope this book can be a ticket for my readers to be able to travel in your emotional world as well.

I couldn't thank you enough for choosing to be on board this journey with me.

Lost

My heart is broken.

All my hope was stolen.

In so much pain, I'm looking for something

to ignite my faith again.

Waiting

My heart is like an open book

but you never care to look

what has been written inside.

Gravity

If my tears drop, it's because of the gravity;

not because of you...

Last Valentine

Last Valentine, we were lying on the ground checking out the stars.

You were saying we would be forever

but now it seems like you couldn't remember.

Our relationship was made to fall apart

and all you do is start a new one with someone else.

My Artist

You are the artist

of my mosaic broken heart.

Being Cursed

Sometimes falling in love

is like

being cursed.

The Beginning

Me loving you

was the beginning of all the sadness.

With You

Stars, moon, sky,

the sound of cricket singing at night,

All of these wouldn't matter

without you by my side.

What Do I Do?

What do I do to shake your face out of my head?

What do I do to sleep well in my bed?

How long do I have to wait

to be myself again?

Made to Be Broken

I hate rain

for it always reminds me of that night,

the night when your promises were made

to be broken.

WORD GALLERY

You have inspired all my sad words.

Someday

Someday you will read all poems of mine

while I lean my head against your shoulder

whispering that you've been the inspiration

of every single line.

Not Capable

I'd been fabulously single

but now I am not capable

of falling out of love.

Never Once

However much I try to forget,

I hate to confess

never once in a second

do you ever slip out of my mind.

The Script in My Head

I mostly write stories

of our relationship in my head

and you, most of the times,

don't follow the script.

Somehow, it's my fault.

Another Girl

It's sad to hear

you singing songs about another girl

while every word of my writing is about you.

A Sad Story in Three Words

He loves her.

I was asked to write

a sad story in 3 words.

Wholeheartedly Accept

I list your flaws

so as to get over you

but it turns out that

I wholeheartedly accept all of them.

If This Was a Movie

If this was a movie,

you would chase me down the street begging me to forgive you.

We were standing in the rain looking into each other's eyes

and my pain would be washed away by your sincere smile.

If only this was a movie... if only this was a movie...

Twenty-Four

I'm 24 years old

and I've been told

I'm a desperate romantic.

I love to read the love lyrics

imagining someone will run through an airport,

chasing me down like the scene in the movies,

hoping that one day somebody will climb up a fire escape

declaring his love like he never does to someone else,

wishing that 'the one' will knock on my door

in the middle of the night expressing his infinite love to me

But all in all,

I'm just a 'DESPERATE' romantic 'PATHETIC' girl

who will never stop believing in 'TRUE LOVE'.

Will you marry my flaws?

23

What Could Have Been

Trying to erase this feeling,

I prepare myself to spend

the rest of my life wondering

what could have been...between us.

Now I know why people drink.

Supposed

Love's not supposed to make you lose yourself.

It's supposed to bring the best out of you.

Fabricated

I'm always attracted to those

who have writing skills

no matter how much they love fabricating words.

Invisible Competition

Every time when you look at me,

I know I am competing with her.

Why Did You...

You had been forcing yourself into my mind

but all you're doing now is say good bye.

Which Is Which

Dreams and reality

sometimes it's good to not know

which is which...

Here the thunder comes

I bet there will be some

kissing under the rain.

Serene sea

wish here were we

not only me.

That raining day

was the first day

your lips touched mine.

A Prologue

Maybe just maybe

a wedding could be a prologue

for a tragic love story.

Wouldn't Be

Without you,

there wouldn't be any word.

Waiting

It's like

waiting for the rain in the drought

waiting for the train when the last one just departed

waiting for someone to have a heart

It's me

waiting for your notification.

A Masquerade Party

All of the masks are smiling at me

while the smirk is being hidden underneath.

I couldn't help but wear that mask too.

Hopefully, mine is more convincing.

Crushed

My heart was crushed

and no one could see the biggest part of it

with their naked eyes.

The Same One

Don't called me stupid

for hoping that the person who fixed my heart

would be the same one who broke it.

AYRENE

They say love blinds people.

Then how come I see the world more clearly

with you by my side?

Just a Dream

The worst nightmare is to wake up

and find out that it was just a dream.

Still Remains

Two months have already passed

and I'm still thinking of you.

Will this feeling last?

This question still remains.

Dear Diary,

Dear diary,

Please don't feel pathetic over my lonely life

and don't tell my parents I'm still awake

in the middle of the night

writing something about a guy

whose heart is as cold as ice

and acts like I never exist in his life.

What's Next?

I thought deleting our chat history

could be the first step to forget you

So, I did.

And now what's next?

Still

A year passed

and I'm still reading

our chat history.

Just Temporary

At the end, you are just a temporary person

who somehow makes me stronger, better, and wiser.

So, thank you.

Poems relieve pain.

47

Would You?

If I forgot some words in the song,

would you sing them back to me?

Forgetting for a While

Lying on the ground

listening to a silent sound,

you and me are painting our future together

and forgetting the rest of the world for a while.

Rather Be

Wanna be in the woods

Need nothing but food

pretty please I would

rather be that way.

Average Me

I'm average,

a bit overweight

and I wanna date

a cute guy on TV.

Dear Santa Claus

Dear Santa Claus,

Why do you have to be so mean?

It seems like you never got the letter I've been writing you for the past two years. Now, I'm gonna give you one more chance. Christmas is two months away; please send a man who will stay in my life; otherwise, I'm gonna tell everybody that you are only in the myth.

Can't Imagine

At first, he couldn't imagine how to live with her.

But now he can't imagine how to live without her.

Lingering

That guilt was lingering

In my head

In my mind

In my heart

all-night-long

Addicted

I want to fall in love

and get my heart broken again.

Just realized I'm addicted to that feeling.

Painted with memories

Looking at an empty room,

she paints every inch of it with her memories

in order to be with him again.

Wondering

Wonder if I'm your last thought at night

like you are mine.

No Matter What

On the way to my dreams,

no matter how hard it seems,

no matter how much I want to scream,

I am willing to fight for them.

I Miss

I miss falling for somebody

even if they treat me like I'm nobody

cause' I'd rather be no one

than be someone with no feeling.

AYRENE

In the mirror stands a girl

whom I don't know anymore...

How to Get Over...

I'm falling in love with the same person

over and over again.

Normally, I love being in love with someone

but how come I really hate myself right now.

Maybe it's because he never notices I'm around.

Could you please tell me how

how to get over him?

AYRENE

And I keep reading our chat history

over and over again...
62

Listen to my eyes,

cause sometimes my smile lies.

Thanks to the rain

for covering the sound of my heart

when you pull me into you.

Someday

Someday I'll be living in the forest

in a cottage made out of cake.

And every morning, I'll be picking up flowers

hoping that I would be like this forever.

AYRENE

I always hated my flaws

until you came along.

Mine

The world ain't fair then for breaking us apart.

but here you are right in front of me again.

Now I'm gonna rewrite the stars and ease your pain

This time nothing can tear us apart

because ever since the start you are mine.

You are mine.

Under the Ocean Dark Blue Sky

Under the ocean dark blue sky

You pulled me into you

and your eyes are holding mine.

We were dancing under the stars

while the wind's playing a guitar.

Your face was moving closer

and our lips almost touched each other.

The way you put my head on your chest

is the moment I know my heart belongs to you.

You can't hide your warmth from me.

I know you're not as cold as you seem.

You say true love has no ending

and I don't want to stop dreaming

what could be between us.

I wanna ask how you feel about me.

Trust me, I wanna do.

But if you don't feel the same too,

are you gonna hate me then?

Let stars be the witness

tonight I almost confessed

I'm falling for you...I'm falling for you.

A Promise Breaker.

With me, he has another occupation,

a promise breaker.

Rhythm of Our Lives

I never feel this alive until I see your smile.

You keep dancing inside my mind

to the melody of my every breath

and I need to confess I wanna know

how the rhythm of our lives are going to be.

Start of Something New?

Two hours before midnight, we are walking down the street

talking and laughing like we've known each other for so long.

Looking at the sky, I don't blame the moon for not shining so bright.

I don't blame the rain for falling tonight.

And I don't blame myself for not having an umbrella

Coz he does... he does... he does...

He raises his umbrella and asks 'could you come a little closer?'

I see he flashes his smile while his hand is on my waistline.

So there you go, we are standing under the same umbrella

and he's still talking about his favorite movies.

I wonder if he sees he's making me crazy.

Thank god it's raining heavily; otherwise,

he would hear something strange.

I never knew my heart could pound this hard.

Hey baby can I ask?

Don't you think this could be a start of something new?

My Favorite Pain

Out of every man I have loved,

you are my favorite pain.

Grandpa

You used to call me your chubby girl

who has the biggest heart in the world.

You always shared your noodles with me

and said it's impossible for me to be thin.

You always walked me to school.

Wonder if you know

you're the coolest grandfather

whose favorite movie is Harry Potter.

Watching T.V. with you is a moment to remember.

My dad told me you used to work for the post office.

You'd been working almost ten hours a day.

Never did you say you're tired.

This was the reason why you'd never been fired.

Right now, you are in a better place.

Somehow, I wish I could see your face.

So, I turned on the computer

and looked for a photo album in my folder.

Then I saw a kind old man

who always taught me not to give up

wonder if you know I can't thank you enough

for everything you've done for me.

AYRENE

Dear all stars in the sky,

Could you do me a favor?

I will never be any happier

If you send my love to my grandpa.

Why Why Why!

I met one perfect stranger in an elevator

and I thought he wanted to smile at me

but he was too shy to do that,

so he walked out of the elevator instead.

And all I could do was sigh

wishing he shouldn't have been so shy;

otherwise, we would make a really cute couple

WHY DO YOU HAVE TO BE SO SHY?!?

WHY WHY WHY

sigh

sigh

sigh

But

Fragile,

But I'm not broken.

Sensitive

But I'm not weak.

Emotional

But I'm not going to give up.

Would You Still?

I wish you had a chance with her.

I wish she would have given you a shot.

I wish she didn't end up with the other guy.

So, I can be sure after all these things,

you will still choose me in the end.

It's a forever goodbye

but when you hear my favorite song,

I hope you think of me.

I'm gonna let this feeling fade in time

while waiting for the day

I completely get over you.

AYRENE

They say that time is the best medicine

but to me it doesn't seem that way

since you've been lingering in my head

over and over again.

She Wishes

She wishes...

wishes to meet someone

who's able to discover the real her

that she has been hiding inside herself...

A Nurtured Wound

The wound you left me

has not yet turned into a scar

and the scariest thing is

I've been nurturing that wound

as if it represented you being by my side.

Suddenly,

listening to the song you sing for her

doesn't hurt me anymore.

It's Not You

I've been believing for years that it's you.

No matter what happens, it's gonna be you in the end.

But now it's not. You're not him.

And I'm not sorry for the time we've had together.

I'm just sorry that it's not you.

I don't think he is able to make me in pain

like you were able to.

85

Sooner or Later

I don't believe in happily ever after.

If you do, could you just describe?

Because to me, it's a total lie.

He will break her heart

sooner or later after she says 'I do.'

Well Answered

I use to wonder what could have been

but that question was already answered...

well answered.

I Travel to...

Sometimes, I travel to get inspiration.

Sometimes, I travel to write

Sometimes, I travel to meet new people.

Sometimes, I travel to broaden my horizon.

This time, I travel to forget someone.

I Do Not Want to Compete

I've been loving him and I know he has a feeling for me too. We could have made it. But I can't stand when loving someone and he has the other in his heart.

The reason he chose me is because nothing is possible between him and her. That's why I chose to say goodbye because it is much more painful to be with someone whose heart belongs to the other, the one that in his eyes, I cannot compete with.

The Time Will Come

The feeling of not being good enough... you feel that every time you are insecure. You are drawn into the universe of 'I'm not going to make it'. And once you are about to give up, some voice in your head tell you not to.

You believe that voice hoping the whole thing will turn upside down, wishing that when that time comes, all of the things you've been through will look like a shit and they will not be able to hurt you anymore.

You might even thank those things or those people for making you stronger than you already were. The echoing of the sound inside your heart says just hang in there.

That time will come.

It's going to.

Almost

I-n-d-i-f-f-e-r-e-n-t

Waiting to Be Alive

Living in a distorted system gradually swallows me whole,

I pray...pray to get out of this place.

I try...try to find a way to get myself back.

And I hope...hope that deep down inside

is still the same old me waiting to be alive again.

Suddenly

Suddenly, laughters last year turn into tears this year.

Suddenly, a cheerful me turns into a painful me.

Suddenly, I need to try so hard to keep myself apart from you.

Suddenly, millions of feelings bursting in my chest at night

just because I can't stop thinking about you.

And all of a sudden...I think I love you now.

I Yearn to Cure

You've been setting me up since the beginning.

Yet I could not help but falling for you.

I should have slapped your face for so long

but I realized that you're not cruel and strong like you pretend to be.

Looking in to your dark eyes, I know there's pain inside.

Underneath that smirk is the lonely life which I yearn to cure.

People say you are a person who is hard to deal.

Little do they know that you have a pure heart,

the one making me start to confess something,

something I never thought I would do...

What If

What if this is a forever try?

What if I always lose this battle?

What if this mountain is too high for me to climb?

A person in the mirror asked me while her eyes filled with tears.

Let's See

At some point, I feel like giving up

And I definitely know what will happen after that

But I'm more curious to know how the whole things will be if I keep going

So, let's find out!!!

WORD GALLERY

I still remember the first day I met you.

A part of me wants to turn back time and experience

every moment with you for the whole four years

all over again.

At first, I thought I would not choose a guy who prefers a sunrise in the morning over millions of stars at night, but now I just cannot wait to wake up at 5 a.m. to watch every sunrise with him.

WORD GALLERY

He is the exception of every single rule I've set.

I write to keep myself sane.

WORD GALLERY

Contact

@ayrenepoetry on Instagram

Don't miss out!

Visit the website below and you can sign up to receive emails whenever Ayrene publishes a new book. There's no charge and no obligation.

https://books2read.com/r/B-A-VOTKC-YZBZE